T0150756

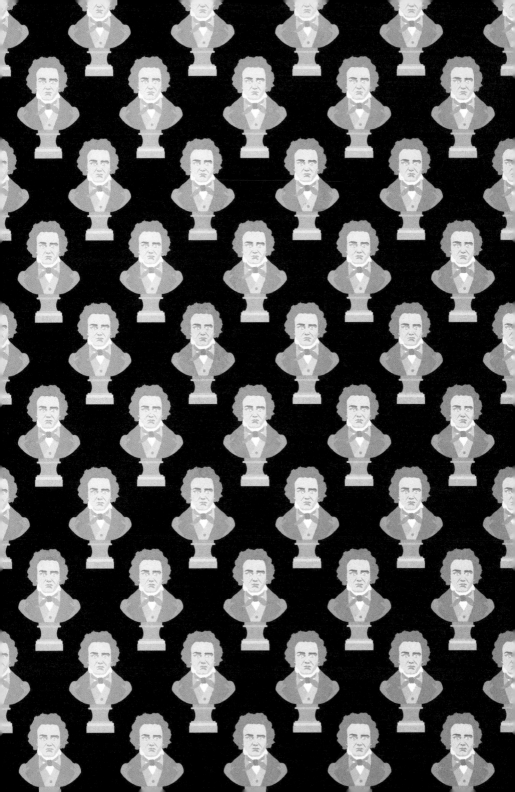

BIOGRAPHIC
BEETHOVEN

BIOGRAPHIC
BEETHOVEN

MARCUS WEEKS

ILLUSTRATED BY
MATT CARR

AMMONITE
PRESS

First published 2020 by
Ammonite Press
an imprint of Guild of Master Craftsman Publications Ltd
Castle Place, 166 High Street, Lewes, East Sussex, BN7 1XU,
United Kingdom
www.ammonitepress.com

Text © Marcus Weeks, 2020
Copyright in the Work © GMC Publications Ltd, 2020

ISBN 978 1 78145 415 2

A catalogue record for this book is available from the
British Library.

Publisher: Jason Hook
Concept Design: Matt Carr
Design & Illustration: Matt Carr & Robin Shields
Editor: Laura Paton

Colour reproduction by GMC Reprographics
Printed and bound in Turkey

CONTENTS

ICONOGRAPHIC

WHEN WE CAN RECOGNIZE A COMPOSER BY A SET OF ICONS, WE CAN ALSO RECOGNIZE HOW COMPLETELY THAT ARTIST AND THEIR MUSIC HAVE ENTERED OUR CULTURE AND OUR CONSCIOUSNESS.

INTRODUCTION

Ask most people to name a composer, and they'll say Beethoven. With his instantly recognizable wild and stormy appearance, he is the popular idea of what a composer should be. But while the name and the face have become icons of Western musical culture, and some of his music is as familiar to us as our nursery rhymes, there is more to Beethoven than meets the eye – or ear. And the man and the myth tell two different stories.

Ludwig van Beethoven didn't get off to a good start. Much to his father's disappointment, he wasn't a child prodigy like Mozart, even though he was bullied into long and hard hours of practice. So, he didn't make the instant fortune that his feckless dad hoped would compensate for his own shortcomings as a musician and breadwinner. Ludwig was good, but not that good. His rise to prominence was a long, hard slog, made harder by having to provide for the family after his mother died. No wonder he was resentful and sullen as a young man, and couldn't wait to get away to the bright lights of Vienna.

"I WANT TO SEIZE FATE BY THE THROAT."

—Letter to F. G. Wegeler, 16 November 1801

He arrived in Vienna in the 1790s, when he was in his twenties. These were revolutionary times in Europe, and the height of the philosophical and cultural Age of Enlightenment. But Beethoven was not so much of a revolutionary – in either his music or his life – as you might expect. Early portraits present him as a cheerful and respectable young man, and his music tends to confirm that impression. He idolized Mozart and Haydn, emulating their refined Viennese Classical style, albeit with a few innovations of his own.

Beethoven followed Mozart's lead in setting himself up as a freelance composer and performer, but although he was not actually employed in the court of some nobleman, he was reliant on aristocratic patronage as he established his career. This relationship, however, reflected the change in social mores: Beethoven was not just a tradesman for hire, but also became a respected teacher and often a friend to those who supported him.

Despite hobnobbing with the aristocrats, Beethoven did have a strong sense of social justice. He admired not so much the revolutionaries who seized power from the ruling class as the people who rose to power as champions of the people (particularly Napoleon, until he abused that power). The idea of the popular hero became a potent metaphor for him when he faced the tragedy of his impending deafness. The prospect of a soundless world drove him to despair, but Beethoven showed his extraordinary strength of character by overcoming it, and finding the inspiration in his situation to develop an innovative musical style, expressive of the indomitability of the human spirit. Revolutionary? Perhaps, but also a logical evolution from seeds planted in his earlier compositions.

Once his deafness had become profound, the familiar image emerged of Beethoven as archetypal temperamental composer, scowling and wild-haired, caring only for his music not his appearance. It wasn't just his hearing loss that led to the thunderous expression and stormy music. Social interaction became all but impossible, at a time when he was dealing with the death of his brother and custody of his nephew, while also managing a now successful career and dealing with publishers, concert promoters and so on. Not to mention a rather stormy love life, involving a string of unsuitably aristocratic young women, without a hope of a happy ending given their social standing.

A combination of Beethoven's severe hearing loss, and the fact that he was past caring what the public expected or thought of him, led to the gradual development of an intensely personal style of composition, and the musical expression of even more profound, universal themes. So, while in outward appearance he changed from angry young man to grumpy old curmudgeon, in himself – and in his music – he moved from optimist, to fighter against adversity, to a final peace and serenity.

Far from the stereotype of the artist in his garret, unrecognized and starving, then buried in a pauper's grave, Beethoven died a wealthy man, and tens of thousands lined the streets at his funeral. He had become a household name in the Western world during his own lifetime. And he has endured as both the most instantly recognizable, and the best known, of all composers.

"AS REGARDS ME, GREAT HEAVENS! MY DOMINION IS IN THE AIR; THE TONES WHIRL LIKE THE WIND, AND OFTEN THERE IS A LIKE WHIRL IN MY SOUL."

—Letter to Franz von Brunsvick, 13 February 1814

LUDWIG VAN BEETHOVEN

01
LIFE

"MY DEFECTIVE HEARING APPEARED EVERYWHERE BEFORE ME LIKE A GHOST; I FLED FROM THE PRESENCE OF MEN, WAS OBLIGED TO APPEAR TO BE A MISANTHROPE ALTHOUGH I AM SO LITTLE SUCH."

—Letter to F. G. Wegeler, 16 November 1801

LUDWIG VAN BEETHOVEN

was probably born on 16 December 1770, in Bonn, Germany

At the time of Beethoven's birth, Bonn was a prosperous city of about 10,000 inhabitants. It was the capital city of the Electorate of Cologne, on the River Rhine, and both his grandfather and father had worked as musicians in the court of the Archbishop-Elector of Cologne. Despite their prestigious employment, however, the family lived in poverty and Ludwig was born in one of the poorest districts of the city.

In an attempt to improve their lot, his father tried to capitalize on young Ludwig's modest musical talent, and lied about his son's age to promote him as a child prodigy. Even Ludwig believed he had been born in 1772, when in fact he was born in December 1770. The exact date is not recorded, but as he was baptized on 17 December, and baptisms were by convention conducted the day after birth, it is assumed his birthday was 16 December 1770.

GERMANY

Also born in Bonn: ▶
Johann Peter Salomon
(1745–1815) German violinist,
composer, conductor and
musical impresario

THE WORLD IN 1770

Europe in 1770 was on the cusp of a time of great change. The effects of the Industrial Revolution were manifesting themselves in Britain, and influencing changes in society elsewhere. Having liberated themselves from the power of the Church, many nation states now wanted to free themselves from their aristocracies too, and revolutions were just around the corner.

ENGLAND

1770

English engineer Edward Nairne is credited with the invention of the first commercially produced rubber pencil eraser.

LEXELL'S COMET

1 JULY 1770

Lexell's Comet passes Earth at a distance of 1.4 million miles (2.2 million km), the closest observed approach by a comet in recorded history.

FALKLANDS

10 JUNE 1770

Spanish marines are sent from Buenos Aires to the Falkland Islands, where they capture Port Egmont and force the British to surrender.

THE ROUTE OF
HMS *ENDEAVOUR*

COOK'S FIRST EXPEDITION
26 AUGUST 1768 TO 12 JULY 1771

England's Captain James Cook (below) sails from Plymouth with 93 men aboard HMS *Endeavour*. In the next three years Cook circumnavigates the globe, viewing the 1769 transit of Venus, discovering the Society Islands, making the first circumnavigation and charting of New Zealand, and becoming the first European to reach and chart Australia's eastern coast.

ITALY
1770

The 14-year-old Mozart, feted as a child genius, gives his first concerts in Italy and composes his fourth opera, *Mitridate*.

BOTANY BAY
29 APRIL 1770

Captain James Cook, on board HMS *Endeavour*, drops anchor in a wide bay, about 10 miles (16km) south of the present city of Sydney, Australia. Cook names it Stingray Bay but later changes the name to Botany Bay due to the variety of new plants discovered there by Joseph Banks, the ship's young botanist. By the end of the voyage, Banks has collected more than 30,000 plants, about half of which are new to science.

ETHIOPIA
14 NOVEMBER 1770

Scottish explorer James Bruce announces that he has found the source of the Nile.

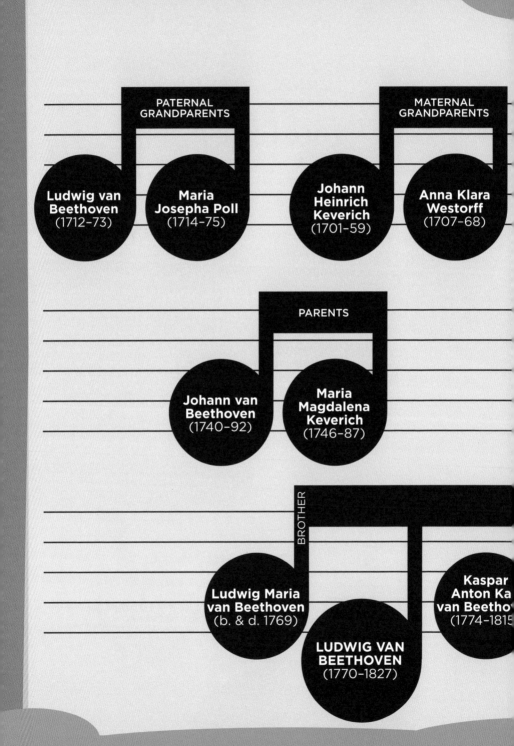

PATERNAL
GRANDPARENTS

MATERNAL
GRANDPARENTS

Ludwig van
Beethoven
(1712–73)

Maria
Josepha Poll
(1714–75)

Johann
Heinrich
Keverich
(1701–59)

Anna Klara
Westorff
(1707–68)

PARENTS

Johann van
Beethoven
(1740–92)

Maria
Magdalena
Keverich
(1746–87)

BROTHER

Ludwig Maria
van Beethoven
(b. & d. 1769)

LUDWIG VAN
BEETHOVEN
(1770–1827)

Kaspar
Anton Ka
van Beethov
(1774–1815

LUDWIG'S FAMILY

Ludwig was the second of seven children born to Johann and Maria van Beethoven, but only he and his younger brothers Kaspar and Nikolaus survived childhood. As the eldest child, Ludwig took on responsibility for the family as his father's fecklessness and alcoholism became more problematic, and was especially protective of his brothers. Perhaps because of this, he never married or had children of his own, but took it upon himself to look after his nephew Karl after Kaspar's tragic early death. This resulted in a bitter and protracted custody battle with his sister-in-law, which Beethoven finally won in 1820.

BROTHER

Nikolaus
Johann van
Beethoven
(1776–1848)

SISTER

Anna
Maria
Franziska van
Beethoven
(b. & d. 1779)

BROTHER

Franz Georg
van Beethoven
(1781–3)

SISTER

Maria
Margarete
Josepha van
Beethoven
(1786–7)

CHILD PRODIGY

1770

Ludwig van Beethoven is born in Bonn, the second of seven children. Only three survive into adulthood: Ludwig, Kaspar and Nikolaus (known as Johann).

1775

He begins music lessons with his overbearing and often drunken father, who later arranges for him to learn the organ, piano, violin and viola with local teachers.

1778

Ludwig's first publi performan billed as a precociou six-year-o performe (although was nearl eight) on his father instructio

Following the family tradition Ludwig took up a musical career, perhaps earlier than he had wanted. Forced into a punishing schedule of music lessons, and paraded as a child prodigy in the mould of Mozart, he had little choice. Attracted by the bright lights and concert halls, and a chance of studying with Mozart, he decided to move to Vienna, but family problems meant that his plans had to be put on hold for some years.

1787

His mother dies and, due to his father's failings, Ludwig has to stay on in Bonn as the breadwinner for the family.

Maria Magdalena Keverich

1746–87

1790

Joseph Haydn (1732–1809), another of Beethoven's idols, stops briefly in Bonn on his way to London, and Beethoven introduces himself.

1792

Extricating himself from family duties, Beethoven returns to Vienna, unfortunately too late to study with Mozart who died in 1791. He takes lessons with Haydn.

1795

Having establishe himself as a pianist, with Haydn guidance a patronage from Princ Lichnowsk Beethoven gives his first public performan in Vienna.

c. 1780

The Organist of the Court of the Elector, Christian Gottlob Neefe (1748–98), begins giving Ludwig music lessons, and encourages him to start composing.

1783

He writes his first published composition, Nine Variations on a March by Dressler, and a set of three early piano sonatas.

1784

Having worked as Neefe's unpaid part-time assistant, Beethoven is employed as a musician in the court chapel of the Archbishop-Elector of Cologne.

1787

Hoping to meet Mozart, Beethoven travels to Vienna for the first time, paid for by the Elector. Soon after arriving, he hears that his mother has been taken ill and returns to Bonn.

When he finally made the move, his reputation as a pianist and composer was quickly established. Sadly, however, any sense of triumph was short-lived, as the horrifying realization of the onset of deafness threatened his future career.

1796

Beethoven accompanies Prince Lichnowsky on a tour, giving concert performances in Prague, Dresden, Leipzig and Berlin.

1798

As he develops his career as a composer, with works including the 'Pathétique' piano sonata, the first signs of deafness become apparent.

1799

Already becoming established as a composer, Beethoven begins taking occasional lessons with Antonio Salieri.

1801

Beethoven's Symphony No. 1 is premiered in Vienna, and he publishes the Moonlight Sonata, dedicated to his 17-year-old pupil Giulietta Guicciardi.

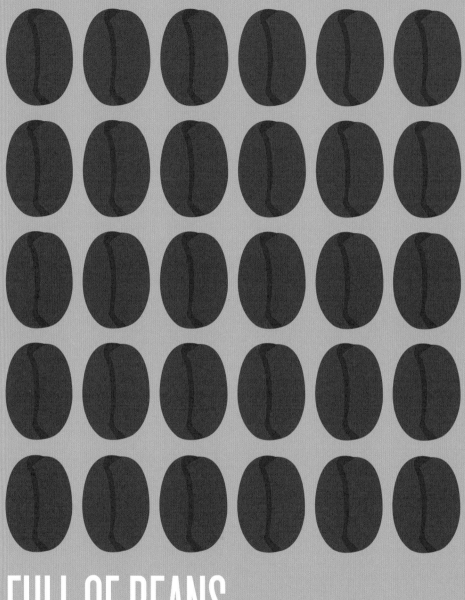

FULL OF BEANS

Beethoven's day began at dawn. His breakfast was always a cup of coffee, prepared by hand. The perfect cup, he felt, required exactly 60 coffee beans, and he would count them out one by one. The coffee was then prepared in his glass coffee-maker. This routine never changed, even if he was entertaining guests.

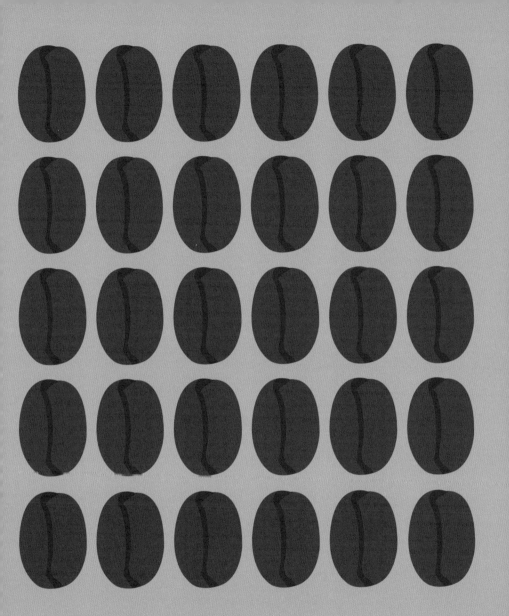

EACH CUP 60 BEANS
CONTAINED 60 EXACTLY

CAUSE

The exact cause of Beethoven's hearing loss is unknown, though theories range from illness to lead poisoning. Some have suggested that after suffering a fall, he stood up to find himself deaf. After his death, the autopsy discovered Beethoven had a distended inner ear, which had caused lesions to develop over time, but the original cause is still unknown.

1798

Beethoven begins to hear a buzzing noise in one ear.

1801

Beethoven confess to friends of his hearing troubles

1799

The buzzing has now become a ringing and is heard in both ears.

1801

Suffering from spells of complete deafness, Beethoven consults a doctor.

1802

Beethoven writes the Heiligenstadt Testament, a letter to his brothers telling of his despair at his deafness.

DEAFNESS

Beethoven's hearing problems began when he was in his late twenties. Fearing it would ruin his reputation, he initially kept his deafness secret. In his thirties, as his hearing deteriorated further, Beethoven was forced to communicate through writing, asking friends to jot down what they wanted to say. Despite his deafness, he continued working, producing some of his most renowned works during this period. By the age of 44, Beethoven was profoundly deaf.

1819

Beethoven is almost completely deaf.

SUGGESTED CURES OF THE TIME

A lukewarm bath with water from the Danube

Balls of cotton soaked in almond oil pushed into the ears

Leeches

Wet bark strapped to the upper arms until it is dry and produces blisters

A mild electric current passed through the afflicted part of the body

1811

Beethoven fails to perform his own Emperor Concerto.

1814

As his deafness worsens, he performs less and less. He makes his final public appearance as a pianist.

1822

Beethoven gives up seeking treatment for his hearing, and instead tries a range of hearing aids such as special hearing trumpets.

LATER LIFE

1805

The relationship with his pupil Josephine Brunsvik intensifies after the death of her husband, but the difference in social status is an obstacle to formal recognition of the affair.

1810–12

Beethoven has a number of intimate relationships, making the identity of his 'Immortal Beloved' in a love letter discovered centuries later a matter of conjecture.

1802

Beethoven leaves Vienna on medical advice, and stays in the small town of Heiligenstadt. There is a marked change in style in his music, heralding the beginning of his 'middle period'.

1806

Ludwig's brother Kaspar marries Johanna Reiss, and later that year their son Karl is born.

1803

Archduke Rudolph of Austria starts taking lessons with Beethoven, and becomes a close friend and patron. Beethoven starts work on Symphony No. 3, the 'Eroica'.

1809

His patrons, Archduke Rudolph, Prince Kinsky and Prince Lobkowitz, agree to pay him a pension of 4,000 florins a year, to discourage him from leaving Vienna.

The latter part of Beethoven's life, in which he was recognized internationally as the foremost composer of the time, was overshadowed by his profound and increasing deafness, family and personal problems, and frequent descents into depression. Nevertheless, in this period he wrote his greatest and most original works, many of them celebrating the triumph of the human spirit over adversity.

1813

Collaborates with Johann Nepomuk Maelzel on Wellington's Victory (the Battle Symphony), to commemorate the Battle of Vitoria, but they fight a legal battle over claims on this work.

1818

Beethoven's reputation has become international. The prestigious Broadwood piano manufacturers of London send him their latest model.

1827

After unsuccessful operations for gastric disorders, and suffering from pneumonia, Beethoven dies on 26 March.

1826

Karl attempts suicide. He and his uncle Ludwig go to stay with Beethoven's surviving brother Nikolaus Johann and his wife on their estate at Gneixendorf.

1820

Gains sole custody of his nephew Karl.

1815

Kaspar van Beethoven dies, and Ludwig and his sister-in-law are appointed co-guardians of Kaspar's son, Karl. Ludwig starts a long and protracted legal case to gain sole custody.

1824

The premiere of his Symphony No. 9, the 'Choral' Symphony, is well received, but is a financial disaster, triggering a row between Beethoven, his backers and the concert promoters.

A CREATURE OF BAD HABITS!

With his wildly unkempt hair and shabby clothes, Beethoven was a conspicuously eccentric figure in the smart streets of Vienna, the epitome of the preoccupied and otherworldly artist. This was due in part to the isolation caused by his increasing deafness, but his mind was also always distracted by his music, often to the detriment of the niceties of life. Although scrupulous about personal cleanliness, he had no time for grooming. His clothes became so threadbare that, one night, friends sneaked into his apartment to replace them. He apparently didn't notice. A similar disregard for housework was put down to absent-mindedness.

Often failed to empty his chamber pot

Had a habit of spitting out of the window, even when it was closed (on one occasion, he mistook a mirror for an open window...)

Often left his meals unfinished

Seldom cleared up dishes after eating

SOAP

Washed frequently and thoroughly, but then dressed in the same shabby clothes

"I HAVE NEVER BEFORE SEEN A MORE COMPREHENSIVE, ENERGETIC OR INTENSE ARTIST. I UNDERSTAND VERY WELL HOW STRANGE HE MUST APPEAR TO THE OUTSIDE WORLD."

—Letter about Beethoven from Goethe to his wife, 19 July 1812

MENS SANA

The cause of Beethoven's deafness is generally thought to have been otosclerosis, the abnormal growth of bone of the inner ear. But an autopsy conducted on Beethoven's body indicated that this was not the only thing that had been troubling him...

BRAIN

'Exaggerated folds' and some thickening, but not enough to cause cognitive impairment

SKULL

Signs of abnormal thickness (contrasting with the 'almost feminine thinness' of Schubert's), and containing excessive fluid

HEAVY METAL

Later research (on a lock of hair) showed there were abnormally large amounts of lead in Beethoven's body, possibly from lead sugar used to fortify and sweeten wine, but maybe from lead used in medication. There was little evidence of mercury, however, which he would have been prescribed had he been suffering (as the rumours suggested) from syphilis.

SPLEEN

Twice normal size, probably the result of liver failure

KIDNEYS

Evidence of calcareous growths, probably from abuse of painkillers (or possibly as a result of diabetes)

ABDOMEN

Swollen by a build-up of fluid, caused probably by liver disease

LIVER

Cirrhotic and shrunk to the size of a walnut, probably from consumption of alcohol, or possibly as a result of hepatitis

PANCREAS

'Shrunken and fibrous'

DEATH IN A STORM

26 MARCH 1827

Rumours abound as to Beethoven's last words. He is variously alleged to have said:

> "I SHALL HEAR IN HEAVEN"

> "PLAUDITE, AMICI, COMEDIA FINITA EST"

("Applaud, my friends, the comedy is over")

In the afternoon, there was a thunderstorm in Vienna. According to the eyewitness account of his friend Anselm Hüttenbrenner, Beethoven died in his apartment at Schwarzspanierstrasse 15, with his fist clenched, to the accompaniment of a loud thunderclap.

It is more likely that his last coherent utterance was said in response to the gift of a case of wine sent to his sickbed by his publisher:

> "PITY, PITY – TOO LATE."

LUDWIG VAN BEETHOVEN

02
WORLD

"I WOULD HAVE PUT AN END TO MY LIFE — ONLY ART IT WAS THAT WITHHELD ME, AH IT SEEMED IMPOSSIBLE TO LEAVE THE WORLD UNTIL I HAD PRODUCED ALL THAT I FELT CALLED UPON ME TO PRODUCE, AND SO I ENDURED THIS WRETCHED EXISTENCE."

—Beethoven, the Heiligenstadt Testament, 6 October 1802

BEETHOVEN'S VIENNA

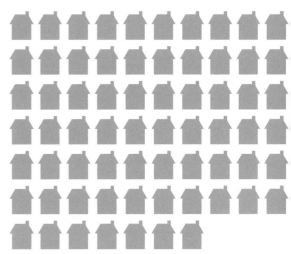

Vienna in the eighteenth century was regarded as one of Europe's most important cultural centres. Attracted by the opportunities it offered him both as performer and composer, Beethoven headed to the city as a 17-year-old, but his first visit was cut short when his mother was taken ill. He moved permanently to Vienna in 1792, and remained there for the rest of his life. During his time in Vienna, it became one of the largest cities in Europe (and the capital of the Austrian Empire), despite twice being taken by Napoleon during the Napoleonic Wars. A permanent resident of Vienna for 35 years, Beethoven satisfied his wanderlust by moving house an average of about twice a year. He lived at more than 60 addresses in the city centre, never far from Vienna's lively café culture.

Most of the 67 **residences Beethoven occupied were located in what is now the inner city, surrounded by the Ringstrasse – a 3.3 mile-long (5.3km) boulevard round the heart of the city.**

WINE AND MACARONI CHEESE

Beethoven had a number of favourite watering holes where he would get away from his piano and clear his head with a glass of Austrian wine and his favourite lunch, macaroni cheese.

551,300

235,000

1790

1850

THE POPULATION OF VIENNA MORE THAN DOUBLED IN 60 YEARS

SCHWARZSPANIERSTRASSE 15

Site of the house where he died — the building he lived in was demolished in 1904.

TIEFER GRABEN 241

One of the first places he lived when he moved to Vienna.

STUBEN RING

PARKRING

MÖLKER BASTEI 8

Beethoven lived here, and it is now one of the Gedenkräume (memorial rooms) open to the public.

KÄRNTNER·RING

CORNER HOUSE AT BEATRIXGASSE-UNGARGASSE 5

Now one of the Gedenkräume (memorial rooms) open to the public.

THEATER AN DER WIEN, LINKE WIENZEILE

Beethoven had an apartment in the theatre complex, which was where several of his major works were premiered, including his only opera, *Fidelio.*

RINGSTRASSE

THE AGE OF ENLIGHTENMENT

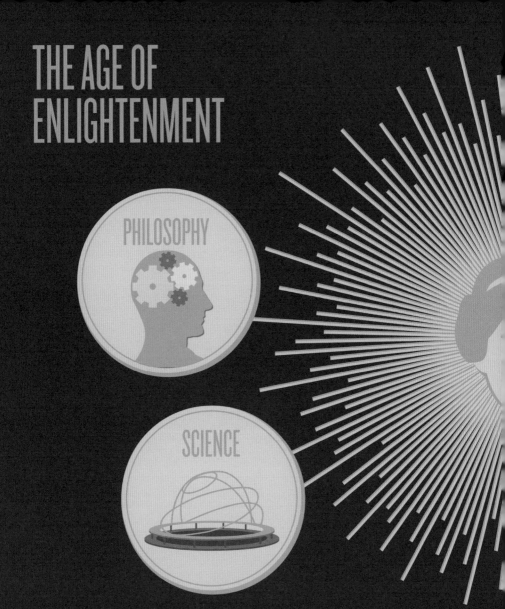

PHILOSOPHY

SCIENCE

The Enlightenment, also known as the Age of Reason, was an intellectual movement lasting most of the eighteenth century that promoted the values of progress, liberty, tolerance and, above all, rational thinking. It succeeded in undermining the old political order, challenging the supremacy of the Church, monarchies and aristocracies, and replacing them with constitutional government – by revolution if necessary. The Enlightenment was well established in Europe by the time Beethoven was born, and had produced composers such as Joseph Haydn (1732–1809) and Mozart (1756–91), whose music embodied the Classical Greco-Roman ideals of formal elegance, and was catering for a growing middle class, rather than being just the province of the aristocracy.

LIBERTY

REVOLUTION

CLASSICAL
MUSIC

TAUGHT BY THE BEST

After childhood music lessons with his father and local teachers in Bonn, in his early teens Beethoven began studying composition with the organist and composer Christian Gottlob Neefe. With his encouragement, Beethoven wrote his first published music. In Vienna in the 1790s, Beethoven sought out the very best teachers. Foremost among these was Joseph Haydn, who took the irascible Ludwig under his wing and inspired much of his early output. Beethoven also took specialist lessons in vocal composition with Mozart's great rival Antonio Salieri, and in music theory with Johann Albrechtsberger.

JOHANN SEBASTIAN BACH

Beethoven idolized J. S. Bach, just as he did Mozart. But there was no chance of studying with him, as he died 20 years before Beethoven was born. Nevertheless, he learnt a great deal from him, especially the art of contrapuntal writing, by concentrated study of his work.

CHRISTIAN GOTTLOB NEEFE
(1748–98)

JOHANN VAN BEETHOVEN
(1740–92)

TAUGHT BY MOZART?

When Beethoven first went to Vienna, it was with the intention of studying with his hero Wolfgang Amadeus Mozart. Although there is no record of the two ever having met, it is quite possible that in the six months he was there in 1786–7, young Ludwig made contact with the 30-year-old maestro and arranged a lesson or two.

ANTONIO SALIERI
(1750–1825)

JOSEPH HAYDN
(1732–1809)

JOHANN ALBRECHTSBERGER
(1736–1809)

MAELZEL'S MACHINES

Sometime around 1813, Beethoven befriended a wily engineer named Johann Nepomuk Maelzel, who called himself an inventor but often simply profited from other people's ideas. One of Maelzel's most notorious scams was the Mechanical Turk, apparently a sophisticated automaton capable of playing chess. In fact the mechanical figure's cabinet hid a human chess master, who made the moves on the board. A pantograph mechanism (a system of mechanical linkages) was used to move the Turk's arm. It wasn't even Maelzel's own machine, but one made by Wolfgang von Kempelen in 1770, which Maelzel acquired in 1805.

THE MECHANICAL TURK

CONSTRUCTOR:
Wolfgang von Kempelen,
Vienna, 1770

THE HOAX:
an illusion with a chess master
hiding inside

CHESS MASTERS INVOLVED:
Johann Allgaier, Hyacinthe
Boncourt, Aaron Alexandre,
William Lewis, Jacques Mouret,
William Schlumberger

DURATION:
84 years (1770–1854)
until destroyed by fire

FAMOUS OPPONENTS:
Napoleon Bonaparte,
Benjamin Franklin

TOURED:
US, Cuba, Europe

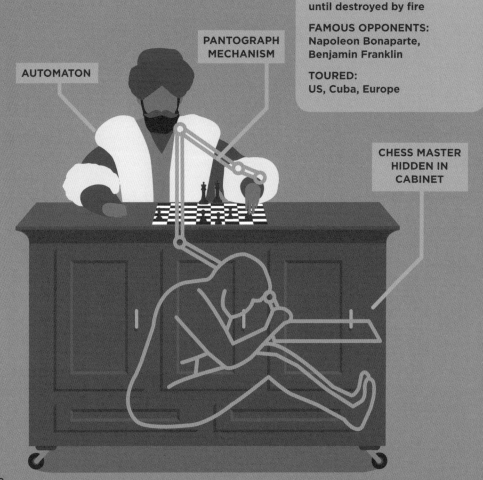

AUTOMATON

PANTOGRAPH
MECHANISM

CHESS MASTER
HIDDEN IN
CABINET

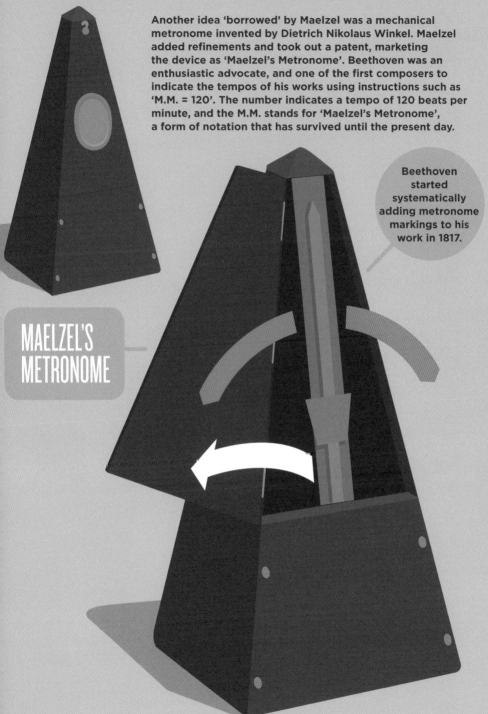

Another idea 'borrowed' by Maelzel was a mechanical metronome invented by Dietrich Nikolaus Winkel. Maelzel added refinements and took out a patent, marketing the device as 'Maelzel's Metronome'. Beethoven was an enthusiastic advocate, and one of the first composers to indicate the tempos of his works using instructions such as 'M.M. = 120'. The number indicates a tempo of 120 beats per minute, and the M.M. stands for 'Maelzel's Metronome', a form of notation that has survived until the present day.

Beethoven started systematically adding metronome markings to his work in 1817.

MAELZEL'S
METRONOME

HAIR COMPOSITIONS

Even the greatest of geniuses are subject to the whims of fashion, and it is possible to navigate the history of the world's most famous composers as they progress from powdered wigs, to bad hair, to fearsome beards...

LULLY
(1632-87)

PURCELL
(1659-95)

VIVALDI
(1678-1741)

HAYDN
(1732-1809)

HANDEL
(1685-1759)

J. S. BACH
(1685-1750)

MOZART
(1756-91)

BEETHOVEN
(1770-1827)

PAGANINI
(1782-1840)

FULL WIGS (BAROQUE, 17TH AND 18TH CENTURIES)

SMALLER WIGS (CLASSICAL, LATE 18TH CENTURY)

BAD HAIR (EARLY ROMANTICS, EARLY TO MID 19TH CENTURY)

WHISKERS (LIGHT ROMANTICS, MID 19TH CENTURY)

BEARDS (ROMANTICS AND NATIONALISTS, LATE 19TH CENTURY)

CLEAN-SHAVEN AND BALD (MODERNS, 20TH CENTURY)

RIMSKY-KORSAKOV (1844-1908)

SCHOENBERG (1874-1951)

STRAVINSKY (1882-1971)

DVORAK (1841-1904)

BRAHMS (1833-97)

JOHANN STRAUSS JR (1825-99)

SCHUBERT (1797-1828)

BERLIOZ (1803-69)

OFFENBACH (1819-80)

WORLD

SOUNDS PROFITABLE

Beethoven's untidy appearance, especially in later life, has contributed to the image many have of him as a stereotypical Romantic, interested only in his art and without a thought for his income. But far from struggling, for much of his career he made quite a comfortable living. Mozart had been one of the first composers to work as a freelancer, rather than employed by the Church or an aristocratic family, but Beethoven was arguably the first to make a financial success of it.

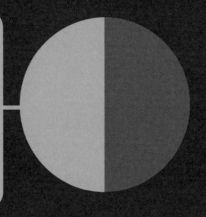

HALF AND HALF

Beethoven made roughly half of his money from publication of his music, and the rest from commissions and other patronage, plus some private teaching.

TCHAIKOVSKY
£5,500

Professor's salary of 600 roubles, plus income from publications.

VIVALDI
£10,000

Salary of 100 ducats a year.

HAYDN
£10,000

Salary of 400 florins, plus board and lodging.

J. S. BACH
£28,000

Salary of 700 thalers and board and lodging, plus some extras from composing and teaching.

The figures given below show the approximate modern-day equivalent of the composers' annual income in their highest-earning years.

MOZART
£100,000

Income of about
4,000 florins from
publications and
performances.

BEETHOVEN
£100,000

Retainer of
4,000 florins
from patrons,
plus income from
publications.

DEBUSSY
£200,000

Income of about
45,000 francs from
compositions and
performances.

THE HEIGHT OF SUCCESS

6'6"

6'0"

5'6"

5'0"

4'6"

4'0"

3'6"

3'0"

2'6"

2'0"

| FRANZ SCHUBERT **5'1"** (1797–1828) | LUDWIG VAN BEETHOVEN **5'2"** (1770–1827) | WOLFGANG AMADEUS MOZART **5'4"** (1756–91) |

1'6"

1'0"

Standing at only 5ft 2in. (1.58m), Beethoven is at the lower end of the scale when it comes to a short history of the heights of the great composers. In stark contrast, Rachmaninov would be first pick for a basketball team, and also had enormous hands that could span 12 piano keys from thumb to little finger (explaining the difficulty of some of his compositions).

| FRÉDÉRIC CHOPIN 5'6" (1810–49) | FRANZ LISZT 6'0" (1811–86) | SERGEI RACHMANINOV 6'6" (1873–1943) |

NAPOLEON AND WAR

Beethoven's most famous contemporary was Napoleon Bonaparte, the Corsican soldier who rose through the ranks to become Emperor of France, before his spectacular downfall and final exile. Napoleon's rise to power coincided with Beethoven's so-called middle period of composition, characterized by its suitably 'heroic' style. Napoleon was, for a time, one of Beethoven's heroes, the personification of all the ideals of the Enlightenment.

1793
Napoleon, artillery commander at Siege of Toulon, defeats Royalist forces

1793
Beethoven begins career as pianist in Vienna salons

1795
Beethoven's first public performance in Vienna

1795
Napoleon defeats anti-Republican forces in Paris

1798-99
Napoleon leads campaign to conquer Egypt

1798-99
Beethoven composes his first set of six string quartets, Op. 18, dedicated to Prince Lobkowitz

1804
Napoleon declared Emperor of French Empire in Paris

1804
Beethoven scratches out dedication to Napoleon in 'Eroica' Symphony

1812
Battle of Borodino: Napoleon defeats Russian army; forces fall of Moscow but has to retreat with onset of winter

1812
Beethoven's 'late period' begins

1814
Napoleon abdicates and is banished to Elba

1814
Beethoven gives his last public performance as a pianist, due to his deafness

1821
Beethoven begins working on his final two piano sonatas

1821
Napoleon dies on Saint Helena

1796-99
Beethoven goes on tour with Prince Lichnowsky to Prague, Dresden, Leipzig and Berlin

1796-99
Napoleon campaigns against Austria

1800
Beethoven's First Symphony is premiered

1800
Napoleon defeats Austrians at Battle of Marengo

1805
Beethoven's 'Eroica' Symphony is premiered at the Theater an der Wien, Vienna

1805
Battle of Trafalgar: French navy defeated by British

1813
Battle of Vitoria: Wellington defeats French army under Joseph Bonaparte

1813
Beethoven commemorates the Battle of Vitoria in his Battle Symphony

1815
Preoccupied with financial and family problems, Beethoven's output becomes limited to lesser, small-scale works

1815
Napoleon escapes from Elba, but is defeated at the Battle of Waterloo and exiled to Saint Helena

The Three Bs

In every era, there are musicians who achieve superstar status. Some, like Beethoven, become legends in their own lifetime, others, like Bach, only get the adulation they deserve posthumously. Conductor Hans von Bülow, a contemporary of Brahms, nominated these three Germans as his choice of fantasy super group, whom he dubbed 'The Three Bs'.

JOHANN SEBASTIAN BACH

1685–1750
Style: Baroque

GREATEST HITS:
1721
Brandenburg Concertos

1741
Goldberg Variations

1749
Mass in B minor

1751
The Art of Fugue

LUDWIG VAN BEETHOVEN

1770–1827
Style: Classical

GREATEST HITS:
1801
Moonlight Sonata

1808
Fifth Symphony

1811
Emperor Piano Concerto

1824
'Choral' Symphony

JOHANNES BRAHMS

1833–97
Style: Romantic

GREATEST HITS:
1868
Cradle Song

1868
A German Requiem

1876
Symphony No. 1
(Beethoven's Tenth)

1879
Hungarian Dances

LUDWIG VAN BEETHOVEN

03
WORK

"YOU WILL ASK ME WHERE I GET MY IDEAS. THAT I CANNOT TELL YOU WITH CERTAINTY; THEY COME UNSUMMONED, DIRECTLY, INDIRECTLY — I COULD SEIZE THEM WITH MY HANDS — OUT IN THE OPEN AIR; IN THE WOODS; WHILE WALKING; IN THE SILENCE OF THE NIGHTS; EARLY IN THE MORNING; INCITED BY MOODS...

"...WHICH ARE TRANSLATED BY THE POET INTO WORDS, BY ME INTO TONES THAT SOUND, AND ROAR AND STORM ABOUT ME UNTIL I HAVE SET THEM DOWN IN NOTES."

—Letter to Louis Schlösser, 1822/3

THREE PERIODS OF MUSIC

Beethoven's composing career can be neatly divided into three distinct stylistic stages. He was inevitably influenced by the music of the age he was born into, and in the 'early' stage emulated (and even plagiarized) his musical heroes. After a hiatus in his output brought about by depression at his impending deafness, there was a marked change. He found a core belief in the indomitable nature of the human spirit, and developed the new musical language – expressing heroism and struggle against adversity – that was the hallmark of his 'middle' period. Isolated from society by his deafness, and able to hear his music only in his own imagination, in his 'late' stage he was free to shun conventions and discover a truly Beethovenian voice, transcending the heroic and aiming for the sublime.

MIDDLE 1802–12

Developing a more expansive 'heroic' style, with innovations including larger forces, longer movements, more expressive harmonies.

KEY WORKS

1802	Sonata in A for violin Kreutzer, Op. 47
1803	Symphony No. 3 in E flat 'Eroica', Op. 55
1804	Opera *Fidelio*, Op. 72
	Piano sonata in F minor Appassionata, Op. 57
1804–8	Symphony No. 5 in C minor, Op. 67
1809	Piano concerto No. 5 in E flat Emperor, Op. 73
1811	Symphony No. 7 in A, Op. 92

EARLY TO 1802

Composing in the Classical style (the refined Viennese style of Haydn and Mozart), while also showing signs of a rebellious streak that reflected the revolutionary times.

KEY WORKS

1784/5	3 piano quartets
1792–4	3 piano trios, Op. 1
1798	Piano concerto No. 1 in C, Op. 15
1798	Piano sonata in C minor 'Pathétique', Op. 13
1799	Symphony No. 1 in C, Op. 21
1801	Piano sonata in C sharp minor Moonlight, Op. 27 No. 2

BEETHOVEN

LATE

Composing in an intensely personal style, in a musical language that is idiosyncratic and challenging, creating a precursor to the Romantic period.

KEY WORKS

1814	Piano sonata in E minor, Op. 90
1816	Song cycle *An die ferne Geliebte*, Op. 98
1818	Piano sonata in B flat Hammerklavier, Op. 106
1819–23	Missa Solemnis, Op. 123
1822–4	Symphony No. 9 in D minor, Op. 125
1825	Grosse fugue for string quartet, Op. 133
1826	String quartet in F, Op. 135

CHANGING STYLE

The changes from one stylistic period to another happened in each case after a period spent away from Vienna: in 1802, Beethoven spent time in Heiligenstadt coming to terms with his deafness, and in 1812 he took an extended break in Teplitz on doctor's orders. Interestingly, during these breaks he wrote some of his most light-hearted works — the jokey Second Symphony in Heiligenstadt, and the upbeat Seventh and Eighth Symphonies in Teplitz.

CASE STUDY:

MOONLIGHT SONATA

KEY DATES

COMPOSED:

1801

....

PREMIERED:

1802

in Vienna,
performed by
the composer

....

PUBLISHED:

1802

The haunting first movement of this sonata is one of the best known of all piano pieces, but it's less than half the story: it is followed by a bright and breezy scherzo, and a furiously tempestuous final movement, the polar opposite of its opening. Written in 1801, it marked a shift from the conventional Viennese style of his early works, and gave a foretaste of the stormy emotions of his later music. It was very much a personal statement, not commissioned by a patron, but dedicated to his pupil Countess Giulietta Guicciardi, who he had fallen for in a big way. His subtitle for the sonata, Quasi una fantasia (like a fantasy), gives some indication not only of the way it was composed, but also its manner of performance, as if improvised. At its premiere, Beethoven played the final movement with such passion, he broke some piano strings.

NAMES

Piano Sonata No. 14
in C sharp minor

Sonata quasi una
fantasia

Op. 27, No. 2

Moonlight Sonata

The nickname 'Moonlight' is not Beethoven's – it came from a review by Ludwig Rellstab in 1832 (five years after Beethoven's death) describing the first movement as "like moonlight on Lake Lucerne".

3
MOVEMENTS

Used on movie soundtracks including *Interview with the Vampire*, *Love Story*, *Persuasion*, *The Pianist* and *Sid and Nancy*.

1st
Adagio sostenuto **(C sharp minor)**
A slow, quiet and haunting movement in a minor key

2nd
Allegretto **(D flat major)**
A cheerful, dance-like scherzo in 3/4 time in a major key

3rd
Presto agitato **(C sharp minor)**
A fast, passionate and stormy piece in the minor key

DEDICATED TO COUNTESS GIULIETTA GUICCIARDI

BEETHOVEN

Although Beethoven and Schubert both lived and worked in Vienna, they moved in rather different musical circles: Beethoven in the concert halls and with his aristocratic patrons, and Schubert giving intimate recitals of his work in the salons of respectable, middle-class Viennese society. They met briefly, and discovered a mutual respect and admiration, both later expressing regret that they had not developed a friendship. When Beethoven died in 1827, Schubert served as a torchbearer at his funeral. A year later, when he became mortally ill, Schubert is said to have asked to hear Beethoven's string quartet Op. 131 — the last music he heard before his own death.

56 YEARS

DIED 1827

ABOUT 720 WORKS

138 OPUS NUMBERS COMPRISING 172 WORKS

9 symphonies

5 piano concertos

32 piano sonatas

16 string quartets

1 opera

STYLE

Evolved from a Classical style to an experimental precursor of the Romantic style.

ICONIC WORK

Symphony No. 9, 'Choral'.

NEVER MARRIED, NO CHILDREN

BORN 1770

SCHUBERT

ABOUT 1,500 WORKS*

*many incomplete

DIED 1828

31 YEARS

1822 The only time the pair ever met.

100 WORKS WITH OPUS NUMBERS

7 complete symphonies
Symphony No. 8
(Unfinished Symphony)

11 complete piano sonatas

About 600 works for piano

Over 600 songs for solo voice and piano

Over 20 string quartets

About 150 part-songs for choir

ICONIC WORK

The *Winterreise* song cycle.

STYLE

A lyrical and tuneful Classical style, but Romantic in sentiment.

BORN 1797

NEVER MARRIED, NO CHILDREN

1888

Both were reburied at Zentralfriedhof (Vienna Central Cemetery).

'EROICA' SYMPHONY

KEY DATES

COMPOSED:

1803–4

....

PREMIERED:

7 APRIL 1805

Theater an der Wien, Vienna

....

PUBLISHED:

1806

4
MOVEMENTS

From the opening, Beethoven defied convention with his Third Symphony. In place of the expected introduction, he gave just two abrupt E flat major chords to establish the key. He then embarked on a first movement longer than most previous complete symphonies, and more complex, more harmonically adventurous and generally more iconoclastic than anything heard before. What's more, it had an agenda. With its 'heroic' title, it expressed the revolutionary spirit of the age, ranging from the courageous, through the tragic, to the triumphant. The 'Eroica' was a turning point, both for Beethoven as he began his so-called middle-period works, and for the history of music, as it lurched from refined eighteenth-century Classicism to turbulent nineteenth-century Romanticism.

NAMES
- Third Symphony
- Symphony No. 3 in E flat major
- Op. 55
- 'Buonaparte'
- 'Eroica'

E flat major is regarded as the 'heroic' key, associated with bold or triumphant music, a convention established largely by Beethoven's use of it for the 'Eroica', and later the Emperor piano concerto.

BEETHOVEN

SCORED FOR:

 2 FLUTES

 2 BASSOONS

 3 HORNS

 TIMPANI

2 OBOES

2 CLARINETS

 2 TRUMPETS

STRINGS

1st
Allegro con brio (E flat major)
Notable for abrupt introduction (not conventional slow intro) of two tutti E flat major chords; and for false entry of the horn before recapitulation section

2nd
Marcia funebre:
Adagio assai (C minor)
Solemn funeral march

3rd
Scherzo: Allegro vivace (E flat major)
Three horns are prominent

4th
Finale: Allegro molto (E flat major)
Set of variations on a theme

THREE HORNS

First major symphony to include three horns (rather than the conventional two).

22 NOVEMBER 1963

After receiving news of the assassination of President John F. Kennedy, the Boston Symphony Orchestra gave an unscheduled performance of the second movement, the Marcia funebre, to honour the death of a hero.

BEETHOVEN IN NUMBERS

138

Of Beethoven's total of 720 works, 138 were catalogued by his publishers and assigned opus numbers, arranged in order of their publication date. Many of the other pieces have been catalogued as Werke ohne Opuszahl (works without opus number) and assigned WoO numbers, arranged by genre.

720

WORKS IDENTIFIED AS COMPOSITIONS BY BEETHOVEN

 32
PIANO SONATAS

 16
STRING QUARTETS

 10
SONATAS FOR VIOLIN AND PIANO

 9
SYMPHONIES

 **7**
PIANO TRIOS

 5
SONATAS FOR CELLO AND PIANO

 5
PIANO CONCERTOS

 2
MASSES

OPERA

CHORAL FANTASIA

VIOLIN CONCERTO

MINOR WORKS INCLUDING SONGS, MISCELLANEOUS CHAMBER MUSIC, PIANO PIECES AND FRAGMENTS:

 49

WORKS WITH OPUS NUMBERS, DIVIDED INTO:

FIDELIO

KEY DATES

COMPOSED:

1803–4

PREMIERED:

20 NOV. 1805

Theater an der Wien, Vienna

FINAL VERSION PUBLISHED:

1814

Beethoven's only opera, *Fidelio*, was written at around the same time as the 'Eroica' Symphony, and explores many of the same themes of heroism and the triumph of the human spirit over injustice. Being a theatrical work, it is more explicit in getting the message across. It is overtly political, and leaves us in no doubt as to Beethoven's political persuasion. His choice of libretto, based on an apparently true story, highlights the iniquities of the old order of aristocracy and repression of the people, and the coming of a new era of liberty, equality and fraternity, with a dash of feminism thrown in for good measure.

NAMES

- *Fidelio* Op. 72
- *Leonore, oder*
- *Der Triumph der ehelichen Liebe* (Leonore, or The Triumph of Marital Love)

CAST

Florestan (a prisoner) **– tenor**
Leonore (Florestan's wife, disguised as a boy called Fidelio) **– soprano**
Rocco (a gaoler) **– bass**
Marzelline (Rocco's daughter) **– soprano**
Jaquino (Rocco's assistant) **– tenor**
Don Pizarro (prison governor) **– baritone**
Don Fernando (a minister of the crown) **– baritone**
Prisoners, soldiers and townspeople

BEETHOVEN

TRUMPET

Beethoven uses an offstage trumpet (often performed from the balcony of the opera house) to announce the arrival of the minister, Don Fernando, interrupting the murderous scene in the dungeon.

PLOT IN A NUTSHELL...

PLACE: Spanish state prison near Seville.

TIME: Late eighteenth century.

PLOT: Leonore, disguised as a young prison guard named Fidelio, rescues her husband Florestan from death in a political prison.

1, 2, 3, 4

Beethoven obsessively wrote and rewrote, creating four different overtures. The fourth and final version, for the opera's 1814 production, is now the definitive *Fidelio* overture. The previous versions are often performed as separate concert items known as the Leonore overtures, Nos. 1, 2 and 3.

PRISONERS' CHORUS

The revolutionary sentiments are summed up in the 'Prisoners' Chorus', an ode to freedom sung by a chorus of political prisoners to the words "O welche Lust" (Oh what joy) – anticipating the climax of Beethoven's Ninth Symphony by some 20 years.

THE NINE SYMPHONIES

The odd-numbered symphonies are widely regarded as milestones in Beethoven's development. They are considered more significant and with greater musical and emotional depth than the even-numbered symphonies. Of his nine symphonies, only the famous Fifth and Ninth are in a minor key, and both of these end triumphantly in the major.

NO. 1 IN C MAJOR, OP. 21

NO. 3 IN E FLAT MAJOR, OP. 55 'EROICA'

NO. 5 IN C MINOR, OP. 67

NO. 7 IN A MAJOR, OP. 92

NO. 9 IN D MINOR, OP. 125 'CHORAL'

MORE SIGNIFICANT

BEETHOVEN

7 — IN A MAJOR KEY

2 — IN A MINOR KEY

NO. 2 IN D MAJOR, OP. 36

NO. 4 IN B FLAT MAJOR, OP. 60

NO. 6 IN F MAJOR, OP. 68 'PASTORAL'

NO. 8 IN F MAJOR, OP. 93

LESS SIGNIFICANT

THE LARGEST ORCHESTRA

Scored for the largest orchestra of any Beethoven symphony, the use of double woodwinds and trumpets, four horns and three trombones, with additional percussion, set the agenda for further expansion by Romantic composers such as Berlioz, Wagner, Bruckner and Mahler.

COMPOSED:

1822–4

....

PREMIERED:

7 MAY 1824

Theater am Kärntnertor, Vienna

....

PUBLISHED:

1826

VOCAL SOLOISTS

soprano
alto
tenor
baritone
(or bass)

CHOIR

PERCUSSION

C

E

E

D

A

B

WOODWIND

H

H

VIOLINS II

VIOLINS I

SOLOISTS

KEY   **Timpani**   **Bass drum***   **Triangle***   **Cymbals***

 Flute   **Oboe**   **Clarinet**   **Bassoon**

The culmination of Beethoven's career came with his Ninth Symphony of 1824. Written on (for the time) a massive scale, not only in scoring but also in ambition, breadth of expression, and even duration, it had an overwhelming effect on contemporary audiences, and has remained an iconic staple of the repertoire. At its first performance, Beethoven was ostensibly the conductor, but because of his deafness Michael Umlauf, the theatre's musical director, discreetly directed the players from the sidelines. At the end of the finale, Beethoven was oblivious to the cheering of the audience, and had to be turned around by alto soloist Karoline Unger to observe the enthusiasm of the crowd.

Beethoven was the first major composer to include voices in a symphony: the vocal soloists and chorus only appear in the final movement.

4
MOVEMENTS

Leonard Bernstein conducted two performances of the 'Choral' Symphony, with its iconic setting of the 'Ode to Joy', either side of the recently breached Berlin Wall at Christmas 1989.

E **E** **F** **F**

BRASS

G

G **G**

J **J** **K** **K** **L**

M

VIOLAS

CELLOS

DOUBLE BASSES

 E Horn   **F** Trumpet   **G** Trombone**   * **4th movement only**
** **2nd & 4th movements**

 L Piccolo*   **M** Contrabassoon*

PATRONS

Most of Beethoven's music bears a dedication of one sort or another, often intended to honour (or flatter) the patron who had commissioned the work, or had given him financial support. Beyond the eponymous dedicatees, there are many compositions of a more personal nature, dedicated to people Beethoven held in high regard, or had a particular affection for. These included his teachers, musicians, friends and pupils, particularly those with whom he had an emotional or romantic connection.

ARCHDUKE RUDOLPH OF AUSTRIA (1788–1831)

Beethoven dedicated 14 compositions, including:
• Piano Trio in B flat major, Op. 97 (Archduke Trio)
• Missa Solemnis, Op. 123

COUNT ANDREAS RAZUMOVSKY (1752–1836)

Commissioned:
• String quartets, Op. 59, Nos. 1–3, Razumovsky Quartets

ANTONIE BRENTANO (and her daughter Maximiliane)

Franz von Brunsvik's daughters THERESE and JOSEPHINE

GIULIETTA GUICCIARDI

COUNT FERDINAND VON WALDSTEIN (1762–1823)

Beethoven dedicated to him:
• Piano Sonata No. 21 in C major, Op. 53, Waldstein Sonata

ANNA MARIA ERDÖDY

DOROTHEA VON ERTMANN

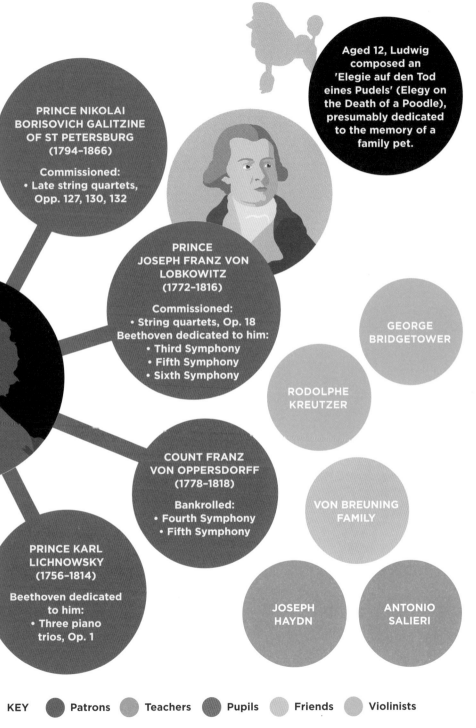

PRINCE NIKOLAI BORISOVICH GALITZINE OF ST PETERSBURG (1794–1866)

Commissioned:
• Late string quartets, Opp. 127, 130, 132

Aged 12, Ludwig composed an 'Elegie auf den Tod eines Pudels' (Elegy on the Death of a Poodle), presumably dedicated to the memory of a family pet.

PRINCE JOSEPH FRANZ VON LOBKOWITZ (1772–1816)

Commissioned:
• String quartets, Op. 18
Beethoven dedicated to him:
• Third Symphony
• Fifth Symphony
• Sixth Symphony

GEORGE BRIDGETOWER

RODOLPHE KREUTZER

COUNT FRANZ VON OPPERSDORFF (1778–1818)

Bankrolled:
• Fourth Symphony
• Fifth Symphony

VON BREUNING FAMILY

PRINCE KARL LICHNOWSKY (1756–1814)

Beethoven dedicated to him:
• Three piano trios, Op. 1

JOSEPH HAYDN

ANTONIO SALIERI

KEY ● Patrons ● Teachers ● Pupils ● Friends ● Violinists

WORK

73

HOW TO COMPOSE LIKE LUDWIG

Beethoven always carried sketchbooks with him, for jotting down ideas. Inspiration came to him when out walking or while eating and drinking at the local restaurants. With his phenomenal musical imagination – the ability to hear the music in his head – he would record the ideas in notation before returning to the piano in his apartment to work on them. Beethoven would often keep making alterations until the pages were barely legible. Sometimes an idea would go through dozens of versions, and then end up almost identical to the first draft.

2. Draw the musical staves yourself.

3. Jot ideas down in pencil as they come to you.

1. Carry a blank sketchbook at all times.

70

sketchbooks survive, along with thousands of single sheets.

5.

da da da DAH!

4. Make the jottings indecipherable.

"I NEVER WRITE A WORK CONTINUOUSLY, WITHOUT INTERRUPTION. I AM ALWAYS WORKING ON SEVERAL AT THE SAME TIME, TAKING UP ONE, THEN ANOTHER."

—Letter to Dr Karl von Bursy, 1 June 1816

LUDWIG VAN BEETHOVEN

04
LEGACY

"WHAT IS BEAUTIFUL IN SCIENCE IS THE SAME THING THAT IS BEAUTIFUL IN BEETHOVEN. THERE'S A FOG OF EVENTS AND SUDDENLY YOU SEE A CONNECTION. IT EXPRESSES A COMPLEX OF HUMAN CONCERNS THAT GOES DEEPLY TO YOU, THAT CONNECTS THINGS THAT WERE ALWAYS IN YOU THAT WERE NEVER PUT TOGETHER BEFORE."

—Victor Weisskopf (1908–2002),
American theoretical physicist

ON THE RECORD

Although Beethoven died 50 years before Edison invented the phonograph cylinder, his music has played an important part in the history of audio recording. Early 12-inch diameter records were made of a noisy shellac compound that played at 78 revolutions per minute (rpm), limiting the playing time to five minutes per side: far too short for a Beethoven symphony or even one movement. The advent of PVC (vinyl) records playing at 33⅓ rpm extended the playing time, and the first one issued in 1931 was a recording of Beethoven's Fifth Symphony. Fifty years later, conductor Herbert von Karajan reportedly advised the recording industry to agree a format for the new compact disc (CD) technology to allow 74 minutes of uninterrupted listening – just enough to hear Beethoven's Ninth Symphony in its entirety.

LONG PLAYER

COMPACT DISC

The first commercial LP (long-playing) record was released by RCA Victor and featured Beethoven's Fifth Symphony.

The format of Sony's first-generation CD was apparently designed to contain an entire performance of Beethoven's Ninth Symphony.

1931

1982

Metal needle in a groove

Laser reading digital audio signal

	DIAMETER	
12in. (30cm)		4.7in. (12cm)

	DURATION	
30min.	15min. each side	74min. 33sec.

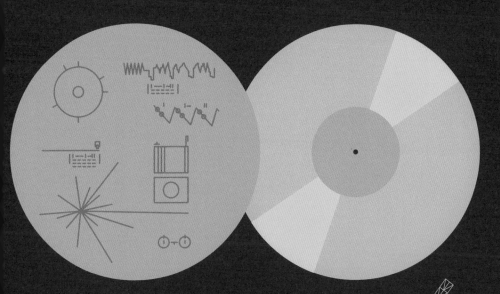

VOYAGER GOLDEN RECORD

The Voyager Golden Record is a phonograph record carried into space on board each of the Voyager spacecraft launched by NASA in 1977. The 12-inch, gold-plated copper disc contains:

115 images

55 greetings in different languages

sounds from the natural world

90 minutes of music

About **15%** of which is Beethoven

The tracklist includes:

—Beethoven's Fifth Symphony, First Movement, the Philharmonia Orchestra conducted by Otto Klemperer (7min. 20sec.)

—Beethoven's String Quartet No. 13 in B flat, Opus 130, Cavatina, performed by Budapest String Quartet (6min. 37sec.)

da da da da

DAH!

—Beethoven's Symphony No. 5 in C minor, 1808

V FOR VICTORY

Coincidentally, more than 30 years after
Beethoven's Fifth Symphony was written,
the rhythm of its opening phrase became the
sequence for the letter 'V' in Morse code: 'dit-
dit-dit-dah'. During the Second World War, the
Allied forces adopted the 'V for Victory' campaign
slogan after British Prime Minister Winston
Churchill employed the 'V' sign as a gesture of
defiance and solidarity. During the war, the BBC
would begin its radio broadcasts with those
opening four notes, played on drums, and so
it became known as Beethoven's Victory
Symphony.

ODE TO JOY

1785

Friedrich Schiller (1759–1805) writes the poem 'An die Freude' ('Ode to Joy').

1786

The 'Ode to Joy' is published. (Beethoven is 16 years old.)

Beethoven chose to set the German poet Friedrich Schiller's 'Ode to Joy' to one of the most straightforward melodies in his entire oeuvre – simple enough for it to be a staple for children in the early stages of learning almost any instrument. This theme is used as the subject of a series of variations that form the last movement of the Ninth Symphony, but it is the full choral rendition of the final stanza of the 'Ode to Joy' at the climax of the symphony that makes it so powerfully memorable. The rousing chorus, associated with Schiller's ideas of freedom and universal brotherhood, caught the nineteenth-century zeitgeist perfectly. It also struck a chord with progressive movements in the twentieth century, when it was adopted as both an aspirational anthem and a protest song.

1989

Student protesters play the 'Ode to Joy' through makeshift speakers in Tiananmen Square, Beijing, China.

1970s & 80s

The chorus is used as a protest anthem by opponents of Augusto Pinochet in Chile.

1824

Beethoven sets most of the text (with minor alterations and some additional text) to music in the final movement of his Ninth Symphony.

1907

American Presbyterian pastor Henry van Dyke uses the tune for his hymn 'Joyful, Joyful, We Adore Thee'.

"ALL PEOPLE BECOME BROTHERS, WHERE YOUR GENTLE WING ABIDES."

—From 'Ode to Joy', Friedrich Schiller

1918

German workers begin a tradition of performances of the Ninth Symphony on New Year's Eve, timed so that the 'Ode to Joy' section welcomes in the new year.

1974–9

The tune is used as the national anthem of Rhodesia, with the words "Rise, O Voices of Rhodesia".

1972

The Council of Europe adopts the melody of the final chorus (without Schiller's words) as the 'Anthem for Europe'.

ROLL OVER, BEETHOVEN

● MUSIC
● FILM
● CARTOON

1956

'Roll Over Beethoven' is written and performed by Chuck Berry. It riffs on the rebellious nature of rock 'n' roll, shaking up the staid music of the older generation.

1963

'Roll Over Beethoven' is covered by The Beatles.

1977

The 25 episodes of Mirek and Peter Lang's British animated cartoon *Ludwig* featured a flying, violin-playing creature with a love of classical music, who played the final movement of Beethoven's First Symphony at the end of every episode and had the catchphrase: "Ah, Ludwig!"

1988

In more of a tribute to Kubrick's *A Clockwork Orange* than Beethoven, the soundtrack to John McTiernan's *Die Hard* is based on the 'Ode to Joy' theme of Beethoven's Ninth Symphony.

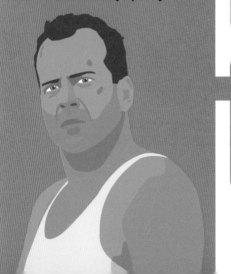

1992

The star of the comedy film *Beethoven* is a St Bernard dog named after Ludwig van Beethoven. The soundtrack features music by the composer as well as Chuck Berry's 'Roll Over Beethoven'.

Beethoven is popularly regarded as the quintessential classical composer, and when Chuck Berry needed an icon of 'square' music to set spinning in his grave, Beethoven was the obvious choice. While Berry merely namechecked the great composer in his lyrics, others have 'borrowed' his music and reinterpreted it more or less affectionately so that Beethoven remains an iconic influence in popular culture.

1969

'A Song of Joy', an arrangement of the Beethoven melody by Waldo de los Ríos, is released by Spanish singer Miguel Ríos. It sells more than 4 million copies worldwide.

1971

Stanley Kubrick's *A Clockwork Orange* features a score by Wendy (then known as Walter) Carlos, including an arrangement for Moog synthesizer of Beethoven's Ninth Symphony.

1977

In *Saturday Night Fever,* a disco version of the first movement of Beethoven's Fifth Symphony, 'A Fifth of Beethoven' by Walter Murphy and the Big Apple Band, is played during a dance contest.

1973

'Roll Over Beethoven' is covered by the Electric Light Orchestra.

1950–2000

In the *Peanuts* comic strip by Charles M. Schulz, the character Schroeder plays a toy piano sometimes adorned with a bust of his hero, Beethoven. Schroeder's playing is often represented by fragments of Beethoven piano scores, notably on 16 December when he pays homage to the maestro on his birthday.

BEETHOVEN'S HOUSE MUSEUM, BONN

Although he only lived there for four years, the family home where Ludwig von Beethoven was born has become one of the major tourist attractions in the city of Bonn. It was a comparatively new building at that time, having been built in the eighteenth century on a site with cellars that date back to the twelfth or thirteenth century. The original baroque exterior has survived, but much of the interior needed extensive restoration before it could be opened in 1893 as a museum dedicated to all aspects of Beethoven's life and work. Several adjoining properties have been acquired by the Beethoven-Haus Association to house the collection, research and archiving facilities, and there is a small hall for chamber music.

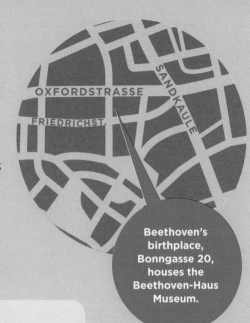

OXFORDSTRASSE

SANDKAULE

FRIEDRICHST.

Beethoven's birthplace, Bonngasse 20, houses the Beethoven-Haus Museum.

01
Beethoven's last pianoforte (made by Viennese manufacturer Conrad Graf)

02
Manuscripts including the Moonlight Sonata

03
Portrait of Beethoven by Joseph Karl Stieler

04
Beethoven's walnut-veneered writing desk

05
The viola he played when he was 18

06
A letter of 1801, describing the buzzing in his ears

07
A selection of hearing trumpets

08
Beethoven's death mask

KEY Ground floor First floor
 Second floor

12 ROOMS ON THREE FLOORS

OPENED TO PUBLIC 1893

200 EXHIBITS

TYPOGRAPHIC BEETHOVEN

EAR TRUMPET

FIFTH

NINTH

SKETCHBOOK

LUDWIG VAN

PIANO

WORKAHOLIC

BONN

BEETH

THUNDERSTORM

SYMPHONY

COMPOSER

DEAFNESS

ALCOHOL

SUBLIME

FIDELIO

PATRONS

ICONOCLASTIC

HEILIGENSTADT
COFFEE
CHORAL
GERMAN
CONCERTO
EROICA
ODE TO JOY
HAYDN
STRING QUARTET
RESTLESS
OVEN
DA DA DA DAH
NAPOLEON
CAFÉS
VIENNA
ENLIGHTENMENT
SONATA
GENIUS
ORCHESTRA
PATHÉTIQUE
HAIR
HAYDN
METRONOME
PASTORAL

IMMORTAL BELOVED

After Beethoven's death, a letter was found among the papers in his desk. It was addressed to his 'Unsterbliche Geliebte' ('Immortal Beloved') for whom the pencil-written pages expressed his undying love. The letter offered no clue as to the object of Beethoven's affections, instigating one of the great historical detective hunts to find the lady. Research in the 1950s determined that the letter had been written on 6–7 July 1812, which helped to narrow the field. Gradually, academics cast doubt on all but two contenders. Beethoven was quite open about his intimate relationship with Antonie Brentano, but she appears on closer examination to have been a dear family friend. On the other hand, his romantic attachment to Josephine Brunsvik (reciprocated, and quite probably consummated) continued over a period of several years – clandestinely, at first because of her marriage, and also after she was widowed, because of the difference in their social status.

THE LOVE LETTER

6–7 July 1812:
Written by Beethoven

10 PAGES

THE CONTENDERS

ODDS ON FAVOURITE
JOSEPHINE BRUNSVIK

3 TO 1
ANTONIE BRENTANO

5 TO 1
GIULIETTA GUICCIARDI

10 TO 1
THERESE BRUNSVIK

20 TO 1
AMALIE SEBALD

100 TO 1
DOROTHEA VON ERTMANN, THERESE MALFATTI, ANNA MARIA ERDÖDY, BETTINA VON ARNIM

OTHER EVIDENCE

13
The number of previously unknown love letters from Beethoven to Josephine Brunsvik written between 1804 and 1809. The letters were published in 1957.

BIOGRAPHIES

Wolfgang Amadeus Mozart (1756–91)
By the time Beethoven moved to Vienna, his musical hero, Mozart, had established himself as the foremost composer of his generation, but died tragically young — probably before Beethoven had the chance to benefit from his teaching.

Carl Czerny (1791–1857)
Aged just ten, Czerny was taken on as a piano pupil by Beethoven. Through their lessons the two became lifelong friends, and Czerny an enthusiastic champion of Beethoven's music, premiering several of his piano works. Inspired by his mentor.

Johann Nepomuk Maelzel (1772–1838)
A wily entrepreneur and engineer, Maelzel built his reputation mainly on other people's original ideas. Apparently a lovable rogue, he and Beethoven struck up a friendship, albeit one interrupted sporadically by arguments over money.

Countess Jozefina Brunszvik de Korompa, aka Josephine Brunsvik (1779–1821)
There was an immediate attraction between Josephine and Beethoven when she and her sister Therese, daughters of the widowed Countess Anna Brunsvik, began piano lessons with him in 1799.

Antonie ('Toni') Brentano, born Johanna Antonie Josefa Edle von Birkenstock (1780–1869)
Daughter of an Austrian diplomat, Antonie met Beethoven in 1810 and they had an undeniably close relationship, putting her in the frame for the identity of his 'Immortal Beloved'.

Count Ferdinand von Waldstein (1762–1823)
One of Beethoven's best known patrons, thanks to the Waldstein piano sonata, Ferdinand had little contact with Beethoven, but was an early champion of his music, and instrumental in securing lessons for him with Haydn.

Julie ('Giulietta') Guicciardi (1782–1856)

Well known in Vienna for her good looks, Countess Julie Guicciardi started piano lessons with Beethoven in 1801, and he very quickly fell for her, but his infatuation was brought to an end when she married Count von Gallenberg in 1803.

Anton Schindler (1795–1864)

As an amateur violinist, Schindler first got to know Beethoven in 1814, and became his live-in assistant and secretary in 1822. After Beethoven's death, he worked as a music teacher and violinist, and published one of the earliest biographies of Beethoven.

Count (later Prince) Andrey Razumovsky (1752–1836)

A Russian diplomat, Razumovsky indulged his love of music by employing a string quartet at his ambassadorial palace in Vienna, and commissioning a set of string quartets from Beethoven, known as the Razumovsky Quartets.

Joseph Haydn (1732–1809)

'Papa' Haydn, as he was affectionately known, took young Beethoven under his wing as a pupil in the 1790s. As the established 'old master' of Classical music, he was a significant influence and inspiration for much of Beethoven's early work.

Anselm Hüttenbrenner (1794–1868)

A keen and modestly successful pianist and composer, Hüttenbrenner was well known in Vienna's musical circles. He was one of only two people (the other being Beethoven's housekeeper) present when Beethoven died.

Archduke Rudolph of Austria (1788–1831)

Rudolph became a firm friend of Beethoven when he took music lessons with him beginning in 1804. They met and corresponded regularly over the next two decades, and in return for his support, Beethoven dedicated several works to him.

Inspiration   Beloved

Friends   Patrons

INDEX

A LITTLE BIT OF BEETHOVEN WENT A LONG WAY...

Among the admirers paying their respects at his deathbed was a young musician, Ferdinand Hiller, who snipped a lock of Beethoven's hair as a memento. It became a treasured Hiller family heirloom, passed down the generations for more than a century, ending up in Denmark during the Second World War. Here, it was given to Kay Fremming, a doctor who was helping Jews to flee the Nazi occupation, and after his death was passed on to his daughter, who eventually sold it at auction in 1994. The buyers were the wonderfully named Ira F. Brilliant and Alfredo 'Che' Guevara of the Brilliant Center for Beethoven Studies at San Jose State University, who subjected the lock of hair to scrupulous scientific analysis, in the hope of gaining some insight into the medical causes of the great composer's death and deafness. Examination showed that Beethoven, amongst his other medical problems, had dangerously high levels of lead in his body, possibly the ultimate cause of his death.

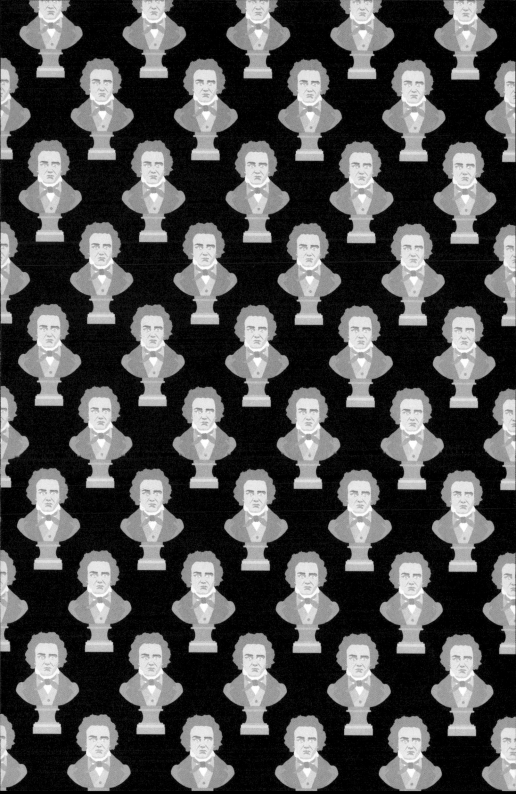

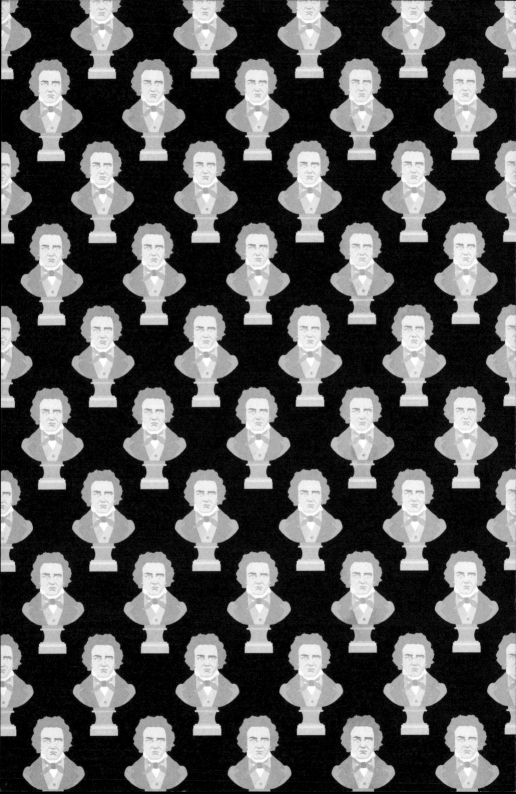